THE

SEQUENCE

OF SCHOOL

TURNAROUND

"A Superintendent's Letters to Principals"

PASCAL MUBENGA, PH.D

Published by Lee's Press and Publishing Company
www.LeesPress.net

Lee's PRESS | *A Premiere Self-Publishing Services Company*

ISBN-13: 978-1-964234-04-5

PAPERBACK

Table of Contents

Foreword

In the challenging landscape of education, where the success of our students is paramount, the role of school principals is pivotal. In this compendium of letters, Dr. Pascal Mubenga, a seasoned practitioner, navigates the turbulent waters of successfully turning around failing schools. Each letter within these pages offers an in-depth look into the profound insights, strategies, and reflections on the noble task of successful transformation. From establishing a core team, identifying goals, fostering a culture of collaboration, and implementing data-driven interventions to nurturing a sense of belonging, the steps outlined here are not merely theoretical constructs but battle-tested tactics honed in the trenches of education. As you delve into these letters, you will find inspiration, wisdom, and practical guidance to embark on your own odyssey of school turnaround. Whether you are a seasoned veteran seeking new perspectives or a novice administrator brimming with passion and ambition, the letters contained herein will serve as beacons illuminating the path toward educational excellence for all.

-Elizabeth S. Keith, Ed. D.
Retired Central Office Educator Board Chair of Franklin County Schools, NC

Since the inception of NCLB in 2002, schools and school districts have been charged with raising student achievement, largely defined by students' scores on state tests. In too many cases, the reputation of schools and school districts, as well as the careers of educators who worked in those districts, have been made or broken based on the performance of these tests. To be fair, one of the pros of the emphasis on student achievement is that it does create attention to the need for schools and school districts to aggressively address and be accountable for the academic successes of ALL children.

The shortsightedness is that over-reliance on standardized, one-shot testing as the primary determinant of student achievement, arguably did not accomplish that goal. Regardless, educators were charged then, and still are charged with navigating that landscape. The extent to which leaders are prepared to lead schools and school districts in succeeding with that goal in mind, is the extent to which public education is being defined. School transformation does not happen in a vacuum or by coincidence.

So, what might be possible solutions, and what are the implications for school leaders as we hone our practice to address the academic needs of ALL students? School leaders need a guide with tried-and-true practices from individuals in the field who have done just that.

In Mubenga's treatment: *The Sequence of School Turnaround: A Superintendent's Letters to Principals,* Mubenga provides many of the tools needed for success. He essentially provides a road map with step-by-step, practical strategies to assist school leaders in what is a noble and awe-inspiring journey—improving and sustaining high levels of student achievement.

Mubenga's focus on building the capacity of effective building-level and district-level teams, his highlighting the importance of collaboration and competence among staff—undergirded with professional development—and his emphasis on data-driven goal-setting to focus the work demonstrate how school leaders can effectively design systems and protocols to support learning communities that can transform schools and school districts.

I commend Mubenga for understanding the importance of those who possess his level of expertise and experience and being willing to put pen to paper and share those experiences with current, upcoming, and developing leaders. It is through sharing the knowledge from legacies such as his, that we make the next generations of educators stronger. Through his manuscripts, Mubenga includes structures that are easily read, practical to implement, and that include common-sense strategies.

Finally, Mubenga's approach of using "letters" as a format to share his experiences is both reflective and informative. This approach is powerful in capturing his personal stories and successful experiences as a school leader. This work provides a chronology of some of his most pivotal successes as a lifelong educator, in a manner to which school administrators can easily relate. We are fortunate to have a legend at this level share his personal journey.

–Dr. Nettie Collins-Hart
Superintendent of Hazelwood School District
2019 Superintendent of the Year
National Association of School Superintendents

Acknowledgments

I would like to express my deepest gratitude to the principals and educational colleagues who have been part of my journey over the past 28 years. Your guidance, support, and collaboration have been invaluable in shaping my perspective and enriching my experiences.

Special thanks to Dr. Stacy D. Stewart, Mrs. Luvenia Foster, and Mrs. Venessa Spearman for your invaluable contributions and insightful feedback. Your expertise and dedication have significantly enhanced the quality of this book.

To my family, particularly Sarah, Angela, and my wife Chantal, thank you for your unwavering support, understanding, and encouragement throughout this endeavor. Your love and patience have been my anchor, enabling me to pursue my passion for writing with confidence.

I am truly grateful to each and every individual who has played a part, no matter how big or small, in the realization of this project. Your encouragement and support have meant the world to me.

Introduction

Over my twenty-eight years in public education, I have had the opportunity to learn from several great educators. Like viewing persons entering and exiting a subway train, one after the other, educators have left the profession without formalizing in writing their invaluable experiences to pass the torch to future leaders. With fewer young professionals entering the field of education, we are facing a shortage of talented administrators prepared to lead our schools and districts.

In an ever-changing world filled with challenges, the practice and methodology of educating future generations is evolving. Assuredly, the needs of working parents correspond with the needs of students being in the care of highly effective leaders in schools focused on quality teaching and learning. An effective master schedule, along with a platform for teachers to collaborate and set goals will continue to be crucial tools as leaders work to properly educate our future generations.

Within the span of my educational career, I have been fortunate to serve in diverse roles: classroom teacher, middle and high school administrator, consultant at the North Carolina Department of Public Instruction, and superintendent of both a midsize and large school district.

My purpose for writing these letters to current and future school leaders is to share evidence-based practices that I have perfected and enjoyed implementing as a successful turnaround principal and superintendent. These practices can be replicated in any educational setting and can also be scaled up and customized to meet the needs of leaders. It is important to note that there are other best practices or tools not mentioned in this manuscript that can also be implemented to transform your school. Nonetheless, I am confident that the 10 letters highlighted in this book, if used with fidelity, will result in significant improvement in student learning and subsequently turning around your school. Equally, district leaders, even though these letters are intentionally addressed to school leaders, you may find some letters contain strategies that are pertinent to guide your district to new heights.

My objective is to share tools that have contributed to my overall success in K-12 education as a school principal and district superintendent Through these letters, you will have guidance at your disposal to change the trajectory of your school or school system. *Leadership matters.*

Letter 1

Establish the Dream Team

Dear Leaders:

As you are in a position to lead your school, I want to take this opportunity to remind you that your college professors were right when they stated you are going to need a team to effectively run a school. I learned this lesson in my first role as a school leader. The selection of your team members will determine your fate as a successful or ineffective leader.

You are the leader of your staff. Your primary responsibility is to provide thoughtful, visionary leadership founded upon reliable and relevant data. Advisably, you should conduct a comprehensive needs assessment of your school and correlate the results with your talents to address the challenges of turning around a low-performing or struggling school. There are many instruments one could use for these purposes. I suggest the use of the SWOT analysis protocol (see Appendix A) to assess both the school and your leadership status. Authentic discussions and reflections, identification of strengths, weaknesses, opportunities, and threats within the school environment, as well as one's leadership capacity, is the first step to turnaround. You must face the facts, no matter how brutal, to lead fearlessly, for this is a requirement for school transformation.

Select your administrative team members carefully. You should choose people who will complement your strengths. I have encountered leaders who were looking for administrative team members who had similar talents or strengths as the leader. This concept leads to an unbalanced leadership team. School turnaround is difficult work and by nature results in the need to engage stakeholder groups in critical conversations. If all members of the administrative team play the nice game and cannot boldly confront issues as they arise, change is avoided. Ideally, these partners will have the same perspective as yours, but in a collaborative environment, your team members should challenge your thoughts enabling you to make well-informed decisions that will move your school forward. Diversity in a team leads to productivity. Without it, the status quo continues to be the order of the day. A different leadership drive type (see Appendix B) is needed for balanced leadership. Trust me, sometimes it can be painful to subject yourself when different views and different perspectives are around your table. The work of turnaround exceeds the thoughts and feelings of one individual, you. Do not take it personally. Your role as a leader is to get the best out of your team for the betterment of your school or your district.

The following are considerations in the selection process of your administrative team:

1. Hire competent members.

2. Hire administrative team members who represent your school population.

3. Hire administrative members with diverse content knowledge.

4. Hire people with a different gender or background.

I believe the above list is just a starting point in the selection of your partners for this rewarding yet challenging work. I hope you will be lucky to hire the right people who can help you accomplish the mission of your school. Competency is paramount in the selection of your partners; however, loyalty is also a critical component in the selection process. In my experience, it has been a challenge to detect loyalty when you meet a candidate during an interview. There are some specific questions you may ask and a careful analysis of candidates' portfolios, but in most cases, it is always a hit or miss to determine a person's level of loyalty. *Good luck with that piece!* Be observant as you are learning your partners and do your due diligence to evaluate and provide feedback to your team members throughout their first month and year.

In terms of distributing tasks with your leadership team, I often see school leaders get burnt out even when they have competent and qualified administrative team members. The problem resides with those leaders who have people who can help them with tasks, but still tend to do it alone. These leaders do not trust others to do the work to their preference or lack the skill set to delegate tasks effectively. Remember, no one can do your job the way you would do it. We are all unique and authentic in our methods of approaching any given task. Great leaders take chances. Distribute leadership responsibilities; if not, you will be burnt out working 24 hours a day, seven days a week.

The principal of a school is considered the commander and chief. In most situations in school or any given crisis, parents and other stakeholders will expect the principal to be the final authority for a matter about the operation of a school; thus, access and availability are paramount in your role. I urge principals to make sure they have fewer tasks or assignments than their assistant principals when distributing tasks to their administrative teams. (see Appendix C). Realistically speaking, even with the most competent assistant principals, when parents are not satisfied with a decision they will seek the principal's involvement. Consequently, being over-tasked with more roles and responsibilities than your assistant principals will negatively impact on your ability to manage day-to-day operations efficiently and effectively. As a principal, you will always do more than your assistant principals. Your duties should not be more than your team. Let me be clear, when assigning roles and responsibilities, weigh the quality not the quantity in determining whether you have fewer tasks than your assistant principals.

I will conclude my first letter by reminding you that it takes a team to get the job done. Do not assume you can successfully run a school alone. Your responsibility as the school leader is to empower and guide your administrative team to an expected end that embodies your school's vision. It takes work, counseling, and sometimes handholding with your team so they can mature. You have the responsibility to build a team with all its strengths and deficiencies. One more note: Please do not hesitate to invite some members of your staff to serve on the interview committee as you select your team members. You need their buy-in and support when making these decisions.

Yours in service,

Pascal Mubenga, PhD

Reflective Questions

1. Do you have the **environmental awareness** to conduct a SWOT analysis of your school? If so, what data is needed? Which stakeholders should participate in this process?

2. Do you possess a high level of **emotional intelligence** whereby you allow a group of trusted colleagues to conduct a SWOT analysis of you with you? These persons would assist you in identifying your strengths, weaknesses, opportunities for improvement, and potential threats to leading effectively.

3. Balanced leadership is a necessity for school turnaround. Too much of anything is unhealthy for a person themselves as well as an organization. Being fully **self-aware** and as a mature leader, consider ways to ensure your ego does not get the best of you when determining the leadership drive type(s) needed in the team member selection process to guarantee your dream team.

Letter 2

Distribute Leadership for Authentic Collaboration

Dear Leaders:

Congratulations! Thank you for reading my first letter. I hope you consider my recommendation and have an administrative team that can support your work. Your task of selecting your administrative team is the starting process of moving your school forward. School improvement planning provides a mechanism for identifying needs and establishing a common approach to meeting those needs at the school level. Effective school improvement planning contributes to overall school performance by:

- Establishing an understanding of the "big picture" of a school's current state, including student achievement, school environment, teacher community, parent community, and administrative issues.

- Reaching consensus across the school community on which needs represent the highest priorities for action, based upon the potential to improve overall student and school performance; and

- Identifying implementation objectives and tasks, including specific targets, effective practices, and milestones required to address the school priorities.

Leaders, you are leading a school composed of new and veteran teachers. Who should you include as members of your school improvement team? I caution you to be careful; the criterion for selecting your school improvement team is not "yes, sir" and "yes, ma'am" folks. Most innovative works are conducted by a diverse, collaborative team.

During my career, I have had both great and terrible experiences in the selection process of school improvement teams. Let me begin with my bad experiences.

My negative experience:

During my first principalship, I was not wise enough to do my homework by listening to all stakeholders. Upon my arrival, I made it a priority to meet a specific person and seek their advice. This individual knew about their informal influence/power on the staff. They had the liberty to advise me on who should and should not be a member of the school improvement team. Some staff members stated that this individual was the only person I needed to know. Wow! To attribute this amount of informal influence to one individual is scary and can either work toward the good or the detriment of the organization. Subsequently, I invited this individual to a meeting in my office. To my surprise, this individual was so confident to provide me with the names of staff to include whom they considered to be the best persons to serve on the school improvement team and the names of those avoided by any means possible. Needless to say, I felt good after the conversation and felt this particular individual wanted not only the success of the school but supported my success as the leader. With my lack of experience, I felt good that this particular individual wanted to help me succeed as the leader of this school. In return, I decided to take their recommendations by inviting those individuals mentioned and establishing a leadership team. Imagine, a team composed of individuals selected from the same clique with the same mindset and lack of forward-thinking...Big mistake! The team echoed and championed the cause of their informal leader. Although I had positional authority, my influence was limited by the informal influencer. It was the difference between fixed and growth mindsets. They were fixed on how the school should operate according to their comfort levels. I wanted more for the children and the staff. I later realized that some talented staff in my school were not around the table when decisions were made. It took a while to adjust and make some changes that were beneficial to move the school forward. Lesson learned. I should have listened to different groups and should have taken my time to consider others' opinions which could have resulted in better outcomes.

Leaders, listening sessions are very important to set a school or an organization on a positive trajectory. You have probably heard 30-60-90 plans in most entry conversations in education. I highly recommend them if you want to be successful in leading your school. Your initial mistakes as a leader can be made at the beginning of your tenure at your school, and some of those mistakes cannot be corrected unless you change environments. Be advised; proceed with caution!

My positive experience:

It was after the first entry mistakes that I learned to implement 30-

60-90 plans: a 30-day plan to gather input from all stakeholders; a-60 60-day plan to analyze data collected; and a 90-day plan to report my findings and recommendations to my staff.

Leaders, when you are appointed as principal of a school, you should have working knowledge of your school's quantitative data. There are some online sites where you should be able to learn about your school. Your district should be a resource for additional quantitative data available at the school and at the district level. Within my first week as principal, I introduced myself to staff and promised to engage them individually through one-on-one meetings, after I had an opportunity to gather and review quantitative data.

I delivered on my promise. The quantitative data collected allowed me to generate pertinent questions to ask my staff in search of qualitative data. My first 60-minute meeting was with my administrative assistant. Through our conversation, I learned about the school's history and culture. Afterward, my administrative assistant set up meetings with other staff members. Depending on the interlocutors, the meetings ranged from 15 to 60 minutes. Appendix D shows two lists: data sources gathered, and questions generated from the data sources posed by staff during individual meetings.

With quantitative and qualitative data in hand, it was time to do a thorough analysis to get a good sense of where the school was and what my strategies would be moving forward. Again, with this calculated process, you can tell that I had a very effective and collaborative team. A good team does not mean that you will have the "yes, sir" and "yes, ma'am" individuals. It was rather a place where all views of the schools were considered, and an environment of mutual respect was created in alignment and fulfillment of the school's mission.

Yours in service,

Pascal Mubenga, PhD.

Reflection Questions

After reading this letter, would you agree with the following as key considerations for the selection of your administrative team?

1. Your team members should be competent members.

2. Your team members should represent your school population.

3. Your team members should represent members of different grades and departments.

4. Your team members should include your loyalists and the ones who are on the fence.

Based upon your knowledge of your school community, what would you consider to be additional considerations starting with the resume?

Letter 3

Recruit and Retain Highly Competent Staff

Dear Leaders:

This job of leading and transforming schools is not a one-person affair. During my tenure in K-12, I have had the privilege of coaching and leading leaders. One thing I always share with principals is that education is one of the few fields where almost every person under your leadership has a college degree. I repeat the aforementioned statement to remind principals that you are not the only smart person in the room. Considering the above statement, school leaders must be strategic, and thoughtful in recruiting effective teachers, by involving other professionals in the selection process.

Even though the main responsibility of recruiting teachers resides in the human resources department, you are the best person to select the best candidates to fit your school culture. Be mindful. Take this task seriously. School reform or transformation starts with the people you recruit into your organization. Approach this task with all due diligence.

My best recommendation is to conduct a round table with the administrative team and some teachers to hear different perspectives when selecting candidates who will join your team. I caution you not to delegate the screening of the candidates to other people. To the extent possible, you should be an active participant in the hiring process from the beginning until the end. Your hands-on engagement in this process is a necessity, particularly if you have a young team and are leading a struggling school.

You position yourself to positively impact your school culture if your teachers have input in the selection of their peers. It is a morale booster and a quick win if you are new in your organization. Your grade level and department chairpersons will feel empowered if they have a voice in the process.

Recruitment of teachers is usually easy in schools that perform well and in a location where teachers feel comfortable dwelling. However, it is a challenge when you do not have meaningful incentives to recruit good teachers. I have some suggestions to share with you that I used in the past.

As leaders, you must consider non-traditional paths for recruitment when recruiting in difficult areas. The recruitment of teacher assistants (TAs) to the teacher program is a good place to start. Some teacher assistants have amazing experiences in terms of addressing student's needs whether academic or social and emotional. In various instances, these TAs just lack the motivation to become certified teachers. I highly suggest collaboration with your human resource department and local universities to guide your teacher assistants to pursue certification. Their experience in the classroom with students positions them to become your potential teachers. Many have exceptional instructional skills and only lack credentials. Another nontraditional pathway is attracting parents and other community members who love to work with students but have degrees in a field other than education. Start a conversation with them; you will be amazed to see second-career teachers or non-educational degree teachers do amazingly if they are given provisional, temporary, emergency licenses. Also, do not underestimate your influence on your current students who need some advice and motivation to consider a career in education. Once convinced, they tend to be loyal and will return to teaching as a way of giving back to their community.

Unfortunately, the teacher shortage is a national problem. This is not to be underestimated. Staff testimonials go beyond just good compensation. Some teachers will consider accepting less pay rather than working in a toxic or uninviting environment. Conversely, a well-compensated district coupled with a good culture can be a great incentive to recruit for your schools.

Leaders, when recruiting, consider all the hours you will spend coaching and mentoring new teachers. Retention strategies are essential, and I will elaborate on them.

Teaching is a very stressful and demanding job. Competitive compensation may attract teachers to the job but is not the sole factor for retention. Simply stated, good teachers will leave your school to work in a neighboring school district despite less competitive compensation. School climate and culture are equally as important as compensation when it comes to retaining good teachers in your school. There are also other factors such as leadership, driving distance, and student demographics that attract and retain teachers.

I know when it comes to compensation, the superintendent, along with the board decides on the politics of compensation. In your role as a school leader, you have a school climate and culture that you can influence to retain good teachers. Nevertheless, please resolve that not all teachers are worth retaining.

19

To promote a climate of retention, everyone needs to feel valued and have a sense of personal and professional accomplishment. I will share seven actionable strategies for your teacher retention plan.

#1: Establish and Communicate Clear Expectations: As the leader, do not be the author of confusion. Without clear expectations, some teachers will do too much while others will not do enough. In this climate, those who meet or exceed expectations will become frustrated, resign, and seek employment where teamwork is a hallmark of the school. Leadership should establish clear expectations about the school environment for students and staff. Articulating policies and procedures to ensure high-quality learning is fundamental to developing a positive climate and holding each person accountable. This culture of high expectations is essential, making progress and learning possible. Policies around behavior, instruction, and high expectations are important for students and families. These clear expectations keep everyone aligned with the overall mission of the school.

Think about where your school is on the cultural journey. How are you using data to inform practices? How are you involving students or advocating for parental involvement? Take note of those efforts and continue to develop ways to improve the culture and climate of the school. As you are adjusting your practice, look deeply at the data to see how changes in your school structure impact outcomes. The administration is responsible for aligning any new instruction or practices to the vision of the school. Be collaborative in your efforts so the school community can speak to the evolving culture of the building.

#2: Foster Positive Work Relationships: Teachers will enjoy working in a school setting where camaraderie is promoted and fostered and tend to have a long tenure in such an environment. In your role as a leader, you should create opportunities for your staff to build and nurture relationships by scheduling social/ professional events that foster relationship building. You have the power and means to promote relationships and resolve differences to establish good working relationships.

#3: Ensure Physical Safety: As much as pay is a key factor for recruiting and retaining staff, the aesthetics and physical safety of a school play an important role in teacher recruitment and retention. For this challenge, sometimes the school systems must make tough choices of prioritizing academic needs and physical upkeep of their facilities. Unfortunately, in most cases, school principals must work with their custodial services and maintenance teams to do the best they can. I have learned to have frank conversations with staff about my limitations to address the physical safety of my building.

Leaders, try as much as possible to engage your Parents and Teachers Organization to acquire additional funding to address the physical upkeep of your building if your school system cannot afford them. In addition to that, work with your most needy staff who require accommodations by relocating them to different parts of your campus. This can promote retention.

#4: Apply Fairness: Make sure you have clear protocols and processes for assigning teachers to students, courses, and discipline. Fair leaders are respected across the board. They are viewed as tough yet consistent with all stakeholder groups. Teachers want to work for leaders who are supportive and apply fairness in the areas of class scheduling and student discipline. All are linked to teacher retention. You should have a clear and transparent process for assigning teachers to courses and students. If it is a practice for a group of teachers to only teach advanced students while others teach average or struggling students, teachers will leave. Like students, teachers enjoy challenges. Many are inspired and motivated by high-level thinking and curiosity afforded them by engaging in academic discourse with advanced students. I know teachers who left schools because they lacked academic challenge and synergy. As leaders, you must give teachers what they need to keep them inspired and engaged at high levels.

Applying fairness is not a momentous task to include assisting teachers with managing student behaviors. When teachers perceive mishandling of discipline by administrators, they will take it upon themselves to address certain infractions and students. If you handle your students' discipline issues with fairness, other minor issues will not in most cases jeopardize your efforts to retain good teachers.

#5: Provide Induction and Support: In general, we have failed teachers in the process of onboarding and providing time for new teachers to get ready for students. As such, I would suggest a differentiated approach to induction based on teachers with education majors versus those with non-education majors. Support for your new and veteran teachers must be ongoing and tailored to different needs. If your staff is properly inducted and supported with professional development and mentoring, you will be able to minimize the risk of losing the asset of your schoolteachers. Induction programs are comprehensive packages of support that help teachers new to your school or novice teachers transition into a school placement and become competent and effective professionals. Ideally, induction programs should last between two to three years so teachers can get to the maturity level required for effective classroom teachers.

#6: Promote Accountability: The accountability factor is detrimental to teacher retention. Teachers who are committed to their profession follow leaders who set clear expectations for the school and hold everyone accountable. If the most effective teachers, who work hard and carry the load for others openly and consistently slack professionals, see the lack of accountability for others, they will experience burnout and leave the school.

#7: Offer Rewards: Whether a person is an intrinsically or extrinsically motivated individual, all persons need acknowledgment for their work. Rewards, which can be praise or materials, should be utilized as a way of motivating them to stay on course in their jobs. As often as possible, praise and reward teachers so that they feel valued and acknowledged for their work. Without any recognition, you may lose teachers despite how well you compensated them financially for their jobs.

Yours in service,

Pascal Mubenga, PhD.

Reflection Questions

As a reflective leader, on a scale of 1 (not demonstrated) to 5 (distinguished), rate yourself on the following success indicators for hiring and retaining the right fit for your organization:

_____ 1. There is diverse staff representation on the interview team.

_____ 2. We have a comprehensive plan for attracting teachers to our school that includes mentoring, coaching, and compensation.

_____ 3. My verbal and written communications are evidence of my clear expectations of students and staff.

_____ 4. My actions are indicative of fostering a positive climate conducive to teaching and learning.

_____ 5. The school environment is aesthetically pleasing and promotes good health and safety.

_____ 6. The results of the teacher working conditions survey along with feedback from teachers indicate that I am known for being a fair administrator.

_____ 7. There is an established on-boarding and support process for new staff members with an evaluation measure toward continuous improvement.

_____ 8. All staff members can attest to the fact that everyone is held accountable for contributing equally to the success of the school.

_____ 9. There is an established and communicated awards and recognition program at my school.

Letter 4

Retreat During Summer Break

Dear Leaders:

I hope after reading my previous three letters, you consider everything shared as common-sense practices that yield great impact when you are operating as a strategic and intentional leader. I urge you to capitalize on summer break to relax as well as use the time to establish structures and processes toward continuous improvement efforts.

Before the 2008 recession, as a principal, I was allowed to travel with my staff to a location outside the district, a place conducive to relaxation and school planning. During the retreat, we focused on accomplishing three tasks:

1) data analysis of the school improvement plan and brainstorming

strategies to meet school goals, 2) evaluation of school structures and processes and how to improve them, and 3) team building and camaraderie. Based on my experiences, a summer retreat for staff embodies the work of establishing clear expectations, collaborative teams, and building relationships necessary for teacher retention.

Retreat Participants

Ideally, the goal is to invite all staff to the retreat, so everyone's input is on the table. Depending upon the size of the staff, this may not be doable. In a small school, you can invite all your staff and pay for lodging and other expenses associated with the retreat. In a large school, I suggest you select your leadership team, with representation from all grade levels and department members to participate. If you follow the guidance shared in Letter 2 (Distribute Leadership for Authentic Collaboration), the persons participating in the retreat are those empowered and committed to developing the road map for success for the next academic year.

Retreat Agenda

Well-planned retreat opening activities are designed to incorporate relaxation, reflection, and team connections (see Appendix F). Furthermore, reviewing the district's vision and understanding how the school improvement plan aligns with the school district's vision is imperative. Unless you function as an individual charter or private school within a K-12 school district, as a leader, you are advised to work within your system's approach (see Appendix G). Additionally, crafting the yearly calendar immediately is indicative of effective planning and money well spent on a working retreat.

Retreat Outcomes

The retreat intends to accomplish tasks as well as build solidarity. It is always important to revisit the school's vision, mission, and core belief statements every three to five years to establish annual school goals and strategies to meet those goals. When you leave your retreat, you should know your school's improvement status and possess your school's blueprint for success.

Retreat Sharing with Stakeholder Groups

In the case of a small school, if all staff members attended the retreat, there is no need to communicate the outcomes to the team. Your focus should be on sharing the direction of the school for the upcoming academic year with students, parents, and other stakeholders. On the other hand, if you lead a large school, the attendees of the retreat are representatives of grade levels or department chairs. Following the retreat, the principal and school improvement team or leadership team members should have a concrete plan to share retreat outcomes with the entire staff. School leaders should prepare a collaborative and formal presentation with retreat attendees to present the message to the staff to garner strong support from all staff.

Yours in service,

Pascal Mubenga, PhD.

Reflective Questions

1. How do you ensure efficiency and seamless yearly transitions where teachers are renewed and understand the focus and expectations for the academic year?

2. After viewing your school's data for the past three years, how could an out-of-district staff retreat to a relaxing environment like the beach or mountains, support your goals in the following areas: establishing school-wide expectations, collaborating without interruptions from day-to-day operations, recruiting and retaining high quality educators, and empowering staff to problem solve toward the betterment of teaching and learning conditions?

3. How can you access the power of partnerships to fund a staff retreat?

Letter 5

Set S.M.A.R.T Goals

Dear Leaders:

I am going to be very direct with this letter. I have been in K-12 education settings for a long time. School leaders are not accustomed to the practice of setting goals. Traditionally, during the summer months, school leaders design their master schedule, hire staff, craft student and staff handbooks, and plan tasks associated with school opening. All of these are good practices essential to the start of a successful school year. Yet there are other considerations necessary for improving learner outcomes. Effective leadership practices are driven by data that inform policies and practices within the school. A well-informed leadership team knows about student needs and current performance, they are positioned to create structures and implement plans that build the desired school climate.

To plan for school culture change, effective leaders analyze data on school attendance, discipline, academic performance, and perceptions of the school community. This information can help determine areas where leadership could use different tactics to support students. School leaders and teachers can use these data points to provide additional support that ensures high engagement for students and their families. Begin this process by identifying the key datasets and setting an explicit, measurable goal for the culture change you want to achieve.

The question I tend to ask school leaders is "Where do you want to be at the end of this academic year? Or in three or five years?" Most of the time, I will hear responses such as, "We would like to be at 80% with student achievement; cut discipline referrals in half, improve student attendance, etc.," After hearing all these good responses, I always tend to ask, "How do you plan to achieve your goals?" I have seen leaders struggle with these questions. I am writing this letter to share with you some best practices on how to establish relevant and meaningful goals with actionable steps.

You have heard the concept of goal setting in various personal and business environments. Simply put, it is the idea of identifying what you want to happen and strategizing how to accomplish it.

There is a plethora of research that affirms that goal setting and measuring student progress are fundamental to not only student achievement but school improvement. I am always disappointed when school leaders are ill-equipped to establish SMART (specific, measurable, attainable, relevant, time-bound) goals for their schools. When it comes to improving learner outcomes, school leaders who are well-equipped to track performance have the edge compared to their peers. The ability to track performance is as valuable for educators as it is for business leaders, doctors, and professional athletes. Yet school leaders often lack formal training in goal setting.

Leaders, before introducing goal setting to your staff, you should first promote a data culture at your school. Without a proficient data culture, goal setting will seem foreign to your staff. To create a friendly data culture, teachers and administrators should seek reliable data to inform their decisions about student learning. For a school to welcome productive data conversations, school leaders should be methodical and tactical because it is a gradual process that requires fostering and modeling. Data exploration, collection, organization, and analysis should precede goal setting.

With a laser-sharp focus on where students are and a clear expectation of where students need to be at the end of the academic year, goal setting gives school leaders and teachers a focus target for the year. The rigorous instructional delivery during the core instruction and appropriate remediation tailored to meet the needs of students have been my practice for over twenty-five years in K-12 schools and I have not fallen short of attaining my goals. I hope you will utilize these evidence-based practices from my tried-and-true experiences to improve teaching and learning conditions under your leadership.

Yours in service,

Pascal Mubenga, PhD.

Reflective Questions

After reading this letter, consider the following to support your goal-setting efforts:

1. Identify multiple data types to review inclusive of learner outcomes, teacher and student demographics, school policies and procedures, perceptions of various stakeholder groups, as well as other important data sets necessary to inform decision-making.

2. Weigh the impact of each toward the success or failure of achieving school goals.

3. Utilize the school improvement team and establish meeting dates to discuss and analyze the data.

4. Share findings with the entire staff and solicit input and support toward prioritizing the work.

5. Set SMART goals at the school, classroom, and student levels.

6. Provide support and monitor for success.

7. Communicate successes and adjust as needed.

Letter 6

Design a Student-Centered Master Schedule

Dear Leaders:

You have learned through your academic training, from undergraduate and graduate schools, that it is a cumulation of several tasks to make schools successful. One sole thing should not be given too much credit for what made a school successful. I will share my bias; leaders who are involved in crafting the school's master schedule and student schedules are positioned to turn around struggling schools.

Consequently, this activity of scheduling staff and students is very critical for the success of your school. Therefore, principals should not completely delegate this task. This activity should be done in concert with data analysis inclusive of teachers' evaluations as well as the use of quantitative data.

Your role as a school leader is to strategically create learning pathways that are critical for instructional planning and academic success for all students. Key indicators for a successful school are the creation of a master schedule that is structurally developed to meet the needs of students, provides equitable access for students based on their ability, incorporates 21st-century content, and integrates digital learning competencies.

The master schedule is driven by your school's data and is the core of teaching and learning. This *Master Schedule Guide* is not designed to be another operational exercise but a fair way to promote equitable learning outcomes through accessibility for all students. The implementation of rigorous core curriculum and instructional practices must be delivered through appropriate time frames and courses that enhance students' ability to achieve at or above academic levels. When students are not meeting benchmark proficiency levels it is a clear indicator of the need for strategic support, resources, and revisiting the master schedule to make instructional adjustments. As I often reinforce this to school leaders, a master schedule is not written in stone; therefore, it can be adjusted as often as possible to meet the needs of your students.

Your master schedule should address the delivery of rigorous, relevant, and research-based instruction to students using the instructional standards and students' current data. In addition to core instruction, you should be intentional to provide an intervention block during school hours that will provide an equitable opportunity for all students to receive personalized support from their core teachers. This concentrated block of intervention time is crucial because it allows time for staff to successfully meet the needs of all students. Furthermore,

35

during this time students can receive personalized acceleration or enrichment. To ensure student success, an effective master schedule should: build leadership capacity in teachers, empower students, increase rigor, and include time for collaboration and engagement with families.

I know for sure that you have heard that there are teachers who are successful in working with advanced students and others who are good with struggling students or those who are performing at grade level. Nonetheless, you should consider each of the aforementioned factors when crafting your master schedule.

Yours in service,

Pascal Mubenga, Ph.D.

Reflective Questions

Professional Learning Communities is a concept that originated in the late 1960s and became more prevalent in the 1990s. Key researchers (Peter Senge, Becky Du Fours, and Rick Du Fours) have books and articles detailing the how and why of its impact.

1. How have you as a leader embraced this evidence-based practice within your organization?

2. If you currently have PLCs established, how do you ensure the overall effectiveness and value-add of PLCs toward increasing student achievement levels, teacher collaboration, and improved instructional delivery?

3. After reviewing the various PLC structures as outlined in Appendix K, what adjustments will you make in your school schedule to optimize this high-leverage strategy for overall improvements in both student and teacher performances?

Letter 7

Establish Professional Learning Communities

Dear Leaders:

In this letter, I am sharing with you a concept that I always referred to as a school laboratory – the Professional Learning Community (PLC). A school laboratory or PLC is a place where teachers and administrators gather to study data, analyze data, review lessons, share best practices, and generate recommendations to improve learner outcomes. Professional Learning Communities (PLCs) are indeed a sacred place. Your role as instructional leaders is to create this cadre of exchange of experiences.

In my 28 years of educational experience, I can assure you that successful schools always have strong PLCs. Common planning is one important ingredient. To create this framework, leaders must be intentional and allocate appropriate times for formal collaboration when developing the master schedule.

It is easier to design elaborate PLC schedules in elementary settings than at middle and high school levels. However, there should not be any excuses if you are intentional with your master schedule.

Modeling and training staff on effective protocols immersed with the purpose and objectives of PLCs is essential for implementation with fidelity. The PLC concept should be taught and modeled. Several leaders have come short of establishing true PLCs in their schools because they did not provide appropriate training and modeling to make them work. Giving staff time to collaborate without appropriate examples will result in a loss of valuable time allocated to improve teaching for learning.

Professional conversations can be challenging. You will find that people are not in the habit of having critical conversations. The proper use of protocols can alleviate the confusion and stress that is often associated with critical conversations. By following accepted parameters, group members can have very focused discussions. Protocols help educators look at student work, artifacts of educator practice, texts relating to education, or problems and issues that surface during educators' day-to-day lives. The result of using protocols to structure the dialogue within these parameters is an increased and shared understanding among group members that can lead to deeper understanding and action. Protocols also may push people into places they have avoided: facing real issues that, resolved, can make the difference between a school that succeeds and a school that fails the students it serves.

Yours in service,

Pascal Mubenga, Ph.D.

Letter 8

Institute Benchmark Protocols

Dear Leaders:

In this letter, I will share with you a very controversial topic depending on what part of the country or world in which you live. There are opponents to formative testing who will not support my recommendations linked specifically to increasing levels of student achievement. Leaders, you have an awareness of your school and district communities. You must use professional judgment when making decisions that impact learner outcomes.

Now, let's begin our study of benchmarking. To benchmark means to evaluate or check (something) by comparison with a standard. "We are benchmarking our performance against external criteria."

Education is preparation for the future. No one knows for sure what the future entails; however, it is customary to have data points that can predict whether our students are prepared for the challenges ahead of them. In several educational fields, students are exposed to standard-based assessment trials before taking the actual assessment to familiarize them with the actual assessment. In a traditional setting, quizzes and teacher-made tests are used to assess the mastery of the subject or standard taught.

A single-day assessment, GRE, or MAT determines whether a candidate for graduate school will be accepted at the university. Similarly, a single-day assessment, the Bar exam, will determine whether a graduate from a law school will have the license to practice law. Lastly, a single-day assessment will determine whether a teacher will be licensed to teach students. Consequently, our society generally avoids taking a risk on a candidate by licensing a professional based on subjective criteria. As a best practice, we need to assess students where they are in terms of standards learned in preparation for the assessment that will determine whether they have mastered skills or standards compared to students in similar grades. Preparing students for that final assessment is not a bad practice; that is what we call benchmarking. I hope I have made my case in support of benchmarking.

One may ask, "How often should I conduct benchmarks within the academic year to determine student readiness for high-stakes testing?"

First, there are two main purposes for benchmarking our students: 1) for formative purposes to assess whether or not students have learned the intended standards and provide feedback so teachers will adjust instructional delivery; and, 2) to prepare our students for the summative assessment which will determine the level of learning obtained during the academic year and compare students with other students of the same grade level.

To prepare students for learning outcomes and properly assess content mastery, you should benchmark your students two or three times during the academic year. If you decide to assess students twice a year, I urge you to give the first assessment mid-year and the second one two to four weeks before the final exams to have enough time to tweak your delivery and prepare students to be successful. If you decide to assess students three times a year, I urge you to administer the first assessment during the second week of school, which provides teachers time to cover some general expectations with students during the first week. The second assessment should be given mid-year, and the third two to four weeks before the final assessments.

A word of caution; benchmarking is only effective if all teachers follow the established pacing guide and are committed to implementation with fidelity. Without adherence to the pacing guide, school leaders are not able to accurately project students' outcomes at the end of the year. Your teachers should understand the 'Why' associated with benchmarks. You need their buy-in to reap the full benefit of benchmarking.

For benchmarking to serve its purpose, school leaders and or district leaders must be equipped with the necessary information. They must know the correlation of items included in the benchmark with that of the State's testing specifications along with the school or district's pacing versus what has been covered by teachers. Conversations regarding pacing and priority standards should happen so teachers understand the link between pacing, planning, priority standards, and the assessment of student learning along the continuum. Conversely, teachers will understand the impact of not following the established pacing guides and items to be assessed through benchmarks that have not been covered and negatively impact student achievement. An alignment of benchmarks and standards taught must be matched to gather a true picture of student academic performance. This is not teaching to the test, rather this is strategic planning for desired standards-based outcomes.

Once the benchmark is given, teachers must receive the results quickly to make adjustments to their instruction. A benchmark result that is given after a week is too late and it is a malpractice.

Yours in service,

Pascal Mubenga, Ph.D.

Reflection Questions

1. How does benchmarking in K-12 education help identify areas of improvement in teaching methods and curriculum design?

2. In what ways can benchmarking assist educators in setting realistic performance expectations for students at different grade levels?

3. What role does benchmarking play in promoting standardized assessment practices and ensuring a consistent evaluation of student progress?

4. How can benchmarking contribute to the development of evidence-based strategies for addressing educational disparities and promoting inclusivity in K-12 settings?

5. What impact does benchmarking have on fostering a culture of continuous improvement among educators and school administrators?

Letter 9

Construct a Comprehensive, Data-Driven Professional Development Plan

Dear Leaders:

A society with education as the foundation yields high dividends for all. Our ever-changing society requires educators to retool themselves to meet the demands and challenges that the profession brings. Many teaching methods from 20 years ago are no longer relevant as students come to schools with different learning challenges and social-emotional needs. Subsequently, educators are tasked to continuously learn new methodologies and innovative strategies to engage students in an animated, social media-driven, globally competitive, ever-changing world.

Districts and schools reaping success develop, implement, and evaluate the impact of a comprehensive professional development plan. Without an intentional plan, leaders tend to provide busy activities and sessions that negatively impact the overarching strategic plan of the district or school.

Yours in service,

Pascal Mubenga, Ph.D.

Reflection Questions

1. How has your teaching approach evolved since the beginning of the school year, and what specific strategies have you found most effective in engaging students?

2. Reflect on a challenging classroom situation. How did you address it, and what did you learn from the experience that could inform your future teaching practices?

3. Consider the feedback you have received from students, colleagues, or administrators. How have you incorporated this feedback into your teaching methods, and what adjustments have you made based on these insights?

4. In what ways have you embraced technology in your teaching? Reflect on the impact it has had on student learning and identify any areas for further integration or improvement.

5. How have you fostered a positive and inclusive classroom environment? Reflect on instances where you successfully promoted diversity and inclusion and consider strategies for enhancing these aspects in your ongoing professional development.

Letter 10

Celebrate Successes

Dear Leaders:

Some folks are intrinsically motivated to respond in a certain manner and can articulate the energy behind their actions. In most cases, students and staff need something to motivate them to continue doing right for their students or themselves. There is absolutely, unequivocally nothing wrong with motivating staff and students to do the right thing. It is your responsibility as a leader to remind and incentivize students and staff to continue pushing forward to meet personal and organizational goals. Recent theories suggest that **intrinsic** and **extrinsic** motivation are not two opposing constructs, but rather two ends of a motivation continuum (Alderman, 2000). The intrinsic/extrinsic motivation continuum represents the extent to which actions are controlled by reward and the extent to which actions are self-determined (Alderman, 2000). A person can engage in activities to simultaneously fulfill both intrinsic and extrinsic goals. For example, when someone chooses a career that is also intrinsically rewarding, working can produce both intrinsic rewards (i.e. interest and enjoyment) and extrinsic rewards (i.e., salary and prestige). As leaders, we must find a way to make school both intrinsically and extrinsically rewarding for our students. If a student is not intrinsically motivated to do well, using extrinsic motivators such as rewards can sometimes prod the student into action. However, using rewards effectively is an art. Sometimes using extrinsic motivators can backfire. As a rule, positively reinforcing good behavior or high achievement is far more effective than punishing bad behavior or low achievement. However, rewards need to be used carefully, since rewards can harm subsequent motivation. In this letter, I plan to share strategies to motivate your students and staff.

Survey your students for their interests:

Leaders, I recommend that you survey your students on their interest in incentives. At the elementary school level, you can design a simple survey that each class will take, and each grade level will compile the data to bring to your staff meeting. Incentives can be uniform across the school, or each grade level may have a preference. At the secondary level, school organizations, such as the School Government Association (SGA) may be assigned the responsibility of working with their classmates to design rewards/incentives systems for the entire school. Buy-ins are very critical to make incentive programs work for any school or organization. A well-planned incentive program would derive the desired outcomes quicker if the plan is generated by students versus a plan generated by teachers or school administration.

Seek or allocate funds to meet the demands of your students:

In my role as superintendent, I strive to provide program funds based on the average daily membership (ADM) number of students to incentivize students. Student incentives have been one of my guiding

47

principles to turn around low-performing schools. Remember this: some students do not work for free, and incentives may be more of a motivator for some groups. Our students should not wait until graduation to be recognized. Every opportunity you get as school leaders, celebrate your students. Here is a combined list of ways to praise students along with occasions/school milestones:

- Verbal Praise
- Write a Note
- Send a Note/Email/Text to a Parent or Guardian
- School Celebration Space
- Class Incentives/Celebrations
- School Dance
- School Success Chest
- Academic Excellence Ceremony
- Onscreen Success or Sharing Success via the School Website or Social Media Platform
- School Sport Competition

Develop criteria to determine the distribution of gifts:

The school improvement team or the school incentive committee should work on the criteria for incentives. The criteria should reflect the school's mission and be tied to student achievement or student morale. The criteria should be generated from a small group and shared for school-wide approval to ensure maximum effectiveness.

The incentive programs for students should promote student morale and student outcomes. The frequency and the intentionality of incentivizing students is an art and should be implemented with students in mind. In the same way, students need recognition, staff also need to be motivated and praised to continue serving students.

School administration should use a team of teachers and staff, preferably a school improvement team, to decide on staff incentives and rewards. Some of the rewards would not be monetary; however, for monetary incentives, school administration should use their general funds and funds generated from fund-raising to meet the needs of incentivizing students and staff.

Yours in service,

Pascal Mubenga, Ph.D.

Reflection Questions

1. How does recognizing and celebrating student success contribute to a positive learning environment within the school?

2. In what ways can acknowledging student achievements enhance motivation and self-esteem among the student body?

3. How does the celebration of student success foster a sense of community and unity within the school?

4. What role does the acknowledgment of accomplishments play in promoting a growth mindset and resilience among students?

5. How can showcasing student achievement positively impact the school's reputation and create a culture of excellence?

Dear Leaders,

School missions and goals will be met when all the letters are scrupulously implemented. There is always a special touch for each school, but the spirit of these correspondences is to help you move your school forward and change the status of your school from a low-performing to a high-performing school.

Respectfully Submitted,

Pascal Mubenga, Ph. D.

Your Colleague in Education

References

Alderman, M.K. & Cohen, M.W. (2000) Motivational Theory and Practices for Preservice

Armstrong, P. (2010). Bloom's Taxonomy. Vanderbilt University Center for Teaching. Retrieved [todaysdate] from https://cft.vanderbilt.edu/guides-sub-pages/blooms-taxonomy/.

Du Four, R. (2004). What is a "Professional Learning Community" Educational Leadership, Vol 61, Number 8.

Appendix

Appendix A

An Example of SWOT Analysis

Strengths: Experienced and dedicated teaching staff, well-established curriculum, strong community support.

Weaknesses: Limited technology resources, outdated educational materials, inadequate teacher professional development.

Opportunities: Integration of technology for enhanced learning, partnerships with local businesses for extracurricular activities, community engagement programs.

Threats: Declining enrollment, budget constraints, competition from nearby schools, changing educational policies.

Appendix B

Leadership Drive Types

Achievement Drive: Focused on accomplishing goals and attaining success.
Power Drive: Motivated by the desire for influence, control, and authority.
Affiliation Drive: Driven by the need for positive relationships and collaboration.
Autonomy Drive: Prefers independence and self-direction in leadership.
Competence Drive: Strives for mastery and excellence in their field.
Purpose Drive: Guided by a sense of purpose and a desire to make a positive impact.

Appendix C

Roles and Responsibilities of Each Leadership Team Member

Elementary School

Principal	AP 1	AP 2
Front Office Staff	Literacy/SS	Math/Science
Instructional Assistants	Duty Rosters	EC & Speech
Safety	Field Trips	MTSS
AP's	Facilities/Rentals	Grades
Coaches & Counselors	AIG	Awards & Assemblies
Professional Development	Specials	EL/RI
Communication/Media	Testing	Discipline
Social Media	Discipline	PD
Community Partners	Custodial Staff	Buses
Walkthroughs/Observations/PDPs	Title 1	PBIS
Planning/Scheduling/Staffing	Teach/Remote Learning	SOAR
Discipline	Cafeteria Staff	Substitutes
Budget	Pre-K	Parent

		Engagement
Curriculum & Instruction/Data & Accountability	Other duties assigned by the principal	Other duties assigned by the principal

Middle School

Principal	AP 1	AP 2
Effective Communication & High visibility	Effective Communication & High visibility	Effective Communication & High visibility
Ensure School Safety	Ensure School Safety	Ensure School Safety
Weekly Walk-throughs	Weekly Walk-throughs	Weekly Walk-throughs
Daily Monitoring/Feedback	Daily Monitoring/Feedback	Daily Monitoring/Feedback
Teacher & Staff Evaluations & PDPs	Teacher & Staff Evaluations & PDPs	Teacher & Staff Evaluations & PDPs
Hiring, Staffing Plan & Job Fair	Hiring, Staffing Plan & Job Fair	Hiring, Staffing Plan & Job Fair
Professional Development	Professional Development	Professional Development
Summer Planning	Summer Planning	Summer Planning
Discipline (Long Term)	Discipline	Discipline
Staff Handbook	Buses	Buses
Weekly Principal's updates	Testing Coordinator	Open House & Orientation Planning
School-wide Math	School-wide ELA	School-wide Science

Data & Instruction PLCs & Department (6-8)	and Social Studies Data & Instruction PLCs & Department (6-8)	Data & Instruction PLCs & Department (6-8)
Teacher Data Talks	Cafeteria Personnel Liaison	Yearbook Supervision
Athletics Games, Dances & Concert Supervision	Athletics Games, Dances & Concert Supervision	Athletics Games, Dances & Concert Supervision
Community Partnerships	Other duties assigned by the principal	Other duties assigned by the principal

High School

Principal	AP 1	AP2	AP3	AP4	AP5
Discipline: Alternative	Discipline: 9th grade	Discipline: 10th grade	Discipline: 11th grade	Discipline: 12th grade	Discipline: 9th repeat
Depart-ments: EC Student Services	Depart-ments: Science CTE	Depart-ments: Math Health/PE Arts	Depart-ments: World Languages ROTC	Depart-ments: Social Studies ESL Arts	Depar tment s: English
Other Key Responsibilities: Field Trips Security & Keys Master Schedule Master Budget PTO & Community Outreach ConnectEd/ PR Fundraisers Leadership Team Facilities Rentals Professiona l Developme nt	**Other Key Responsibilities:** Master Schedule Transporta tion CERT & Safety Drills AED Monitorin g Substitutes Observatio n Master Calendar Duty Schedules Backup Testing Coordinat or	**Other Key Responsibilities:** Master Schedule MTSS & Interventio n Team Restorativ e Practices Graduatio n EC Backup Testing Coordinat or Custodian s	**Other Key Responsibilities:** Work Orders Restorativ e Practices Student Parking Transporta tion Backup	**Other Key Responsibilities:** Master Schedule Textbooks Peer Mediation AP Program Online Learning & Credit Recovery Middle School Transition Master Calendar of Events PGC Substitute Backup	**Other Key Responsibilities:** Obser vation s Repea t 9th Grade rs

ALL:
- Observations and Walkthroughs
- Athletic & Arts Events
- Faculty Meetings
- IEP and Manifestation Meetings
- Handbooks
- Awards and Recognition
- Discipline and Classroom Management
- Data Analysis

Appendix D

Data Collection

Table 1: A list of quantitative data sought to learn about the school.

Achievement Data
Demographic Data
Education/Program Data
Perception Data
Discipline Data
Attendance Data
Teacher Turnover Data
Dropout Data
Absenteeism Data

Table 2: Questions Posed to Staff During Individual Meetings

What do parents and community members say about our school?
What factors may be preventing parents from different races, ethnicities, or cultures from helping their children learn?
How ready and equipped is our school to address issues of diversities?
What is the process of scheduling students in advanced or

honors classes?
How is our school ranked compared to other schools in the district?
Why do teachers come/leave our school?
How might our attendance and chronic absenteeism rates differ by student group?
Is our school safe for students and staff?
Why did you choose to work here?
What do I need to do to help our school move forward?

Appendix E

Induction Ideas

Induction	Support
For non-teaching majors	• A weekly orientation prior to the returning of students that includes sharing of the state standards, curriculum materials, pacing guides and lesson planning. • A structure for modeling effective teaching during in-services and mentoring for 3 years. • Numerous opportunities for inductees to visit demonstration classrooms taught by successful and experienced teachers. • Support with additional classes and tests in order to meet the licensure requirements.
For education majors	• Three days of orientation prior to the returning of students. Time to receive guidance from the district and school level administrators and get the classroom ready for students.

	<ul><li>A structure for modeling effective teaching during in-services and mentoring for 3 years.</li><li>Numerous opportunities for inductees to visit demonstration classrooms taught by successful and experienced teachers.</li></ul>

Appendix F

Leadership Retreat Agenda Example

HAPPY HIGH SCHOOL OPENING FACULTY RETREAT

August 1st	
11:00 am	Welcome
	Introductions
	Celebrations
	Team Building
12:30 pm	Lunch
1:30 pm	Team Building
	Reflection Activity
4:00 pm	Break – Check-in to lodging facility
5:00 pm	Dinner / Expectations
	Staff Bonding
August 2nd	
8:30 am	Breakfast
9:20 am	Keynote Speaker
9:50 am	Break – Check-out of lodging facility

10:05 am	Breakout Groups
12:00 pm	Lunch
1:15 pm	Beginning of School Charge

An Example of a Document Derived from a Summer Staff Retreat

Happy High School 2021/2022 Social Contract

1. High Student Performance

    a. Growth mindset

    b. Data (Anything needed to help teachers help students to be successful)

2. Reflection

3. Protected Time

    a. Protected time (Planning is respected if we shift back to virtual still have protected time)

4. Community-Communication

    a. Communicate with other teachers to help support students

    b. Communicate with families

    c. Community engagement/parental support

    d. Timely Communication

5. Trust in our ability as professionals

    a. Allow us to be professionals

    b. Flexibility

6. Access to resources, technology, and communication

7. Culture of safety* (with clear expectations of COVID protocols)

8. Support and understanding (from admin and one another)

9. Participation—Be a part of the school

10. Ask for help

Appendix G

Sample Retreat Agenda

Each component of these cyclical elements was discussed in length and strategies to address them were elaborated to improve student outcomes.

Appendix H

How to Analyze Data and Set Goals

Data Exploration

This task should not reside with one person or within one department. To gain input from the broader school community, leaders should invite the entire staff to engage in a brainstorming session on what data they should make available about curriculum and instruction. Before staff engagement, do your due diligence to research adequate resources and gain access to websites and venues that are staff members who are not well versed in data culture. These are questions I would ask my staff to prompt the conversation:

- How do we know whether our students are learning?

- What data should we use to determine whether our students are learning?

- Is it appropriate to compare our students with other students in the district or the state?

- What data can we use to compare our students' learning with that of their peers?

- Can we share websites and other venues where we find data about our students?

Data Collection and Organization

For data to make sense and be readily available for staff use, school leaders should empower a data-savvy staff member to organize their school data in a way that makes data understandable to their staff. Tables 1 and 2 depict how schools should organize data.

Table 1: Elementary School Data Collection Sample

Data Profile: Happy Elementary School

School Overview

Student Enrollment	2015-2016	2016-2017	2017-2018	2018-2019
Total Enrollment (month 2)	853	682	659	664
Attendance	95.4	94.3	94.3	93.8

Demographic Makeup % (#)	2015-2016	2016-2017	2017-2018	2018-2019
American Indian	0.0% (0)	0.0% (0)	0.0% (0)	0.0% (0)
Asian	2.0% (13)	2.3% (16)	2.3% (15)	1.8% (12)
Black	54.4% (355)	53.4% (364)	53.6% (352)	53.2% (353)
Hispanic	35.4% (291)	35.6% (243)	35.7% (235)	35.4% (235)
Pacific Islander	0.0% (0)	0.0% (0)	0.2% (1)	0.2% (2)
White	6.3% (41)	6.3% (43)	4.7% (31)	5.3% (35)
Two or More Races	2.0% (13)	2.3% (16)	3.8% (24)	4.2% (28)

Demographic Makeup % (#)	2015-2016	2016-2017	2017-2018	2018-2019
Economically Disadvantaged	100.0% (682)	99.0% (695)	98.8% (658)	98.8% (659)
Limited English Proficiency	22.9% (150)	23.8% (165)	22.5% (140)	22.1% (140)
Students With Disabilities	11.0% (72)	11.0% (76)	10.3% (67)	11.8% (77)
Academically Intellectually Gifted	4.0% (26)	2.3% (16)	2.2% (14)	1.5% (10)

Suspensions

Suspensions (Short-term)	2015-2016	2016-2017	2017-2018	2018-2019
# of Students OSS	31	66	91	52
% of Students OSS	4.7	9.5	14.0	7.9
# of OSS	51	114	235	74

Suspensions (Restorative Practices)	2015-2016	2016-2017	2017-2018	2018-2019
# of Students RP	2	5	5	25
% of Students RP	0.3	0.7	0.8	3.8
# of RP	3	6	6	36

School Climate

Teacher Working Conditions	2015-2016	2016-2017	2017-2018	2018-2019
Teacher Working Conditions (TWC)-Overall	84.3	N/A	77.8	82.0
Teacher Working Conditions Response Rate	100.0	N/A	100.0	90.0

Student Climate	2015-2016	2016-2017	2017-2018	2018-2019
Student Climate - Overall	79.0	76.0	93.0	86.0
Student Climate Response Rate	108.2	101.1	94.0	97.0

Teacher Turnover Rate	2015-2016	2016-2017	2017-2018	2018-2019
	10.2	15.5	15.1	TBD

Student Achievement

3rd Grade: End-of-Grade (GLP/CCR)	2015-2016	2016-2017	2017-2018	2018-2019
Reading	44.3/26.8	39.8/29.3	32.0/20.5	28.7/17.6
Math	46.4/32.0	41.5/31.7	55.7/37.7	50.7/30.9

Performance Composite Overall	2015-2016	2016-2017	2017-2018	2018-2019
GLP/CCR	44.5/32.1	44.3/29.6	49.7/35.1	43.2/29.6

4th Grade: End-of-Grade (GLP/CCR)	2015-2016	2016-2017	2017-2018	2018-2019
Reading	36.1/25.9	35.5/20.6	44.4/28.6	32.8/20.5
Math	39.8/29.6	37.0/24.1	50.8/38.9	28.7/15.6

Growth Index	2015-2016	2016-2017	2017-2018	2018-2019
	Met/+1.1	Not Met/-2.2	Exceeded/+2.6	Met/-0.2

5th Grade: End-of-Grade (GLP/CCR)	2015-2016	2016-2017	2017-2018	2018-2019
Reading	29.5/17.9	39.8/20.5	40.0/26.5	38.9/26.9
Math	40.0/30.5	43.8/30.3	44.9/32.7	47.2/29.6
Science	77.7/63.6	78.7/52.8	83.7/64.3	80.6/72.2

School Performance Grade	2015-2016	2016-2017	2017-2018	2018-2019
	52/D	49/D	60/C	51/D

English Learner Progress (#/% Prof.)	2015-2016	2016-2017	2017-2018	2018-2019
	N/A	N/A	92/63.9	61/43.3

Table 2. Middle School Data Collection Sample

Data Profile: Happy Middle School

School Overview

Student Enrollment	2015-2016	2016-2017	2017-2018	2018-2019		Demographic Makeup % (#)	2015-2016	2016-2017	2017-2018	2018-2019
Total Enrollment (month 2)	1001	926	858	934		Economically Disadvantaged	71.0% (659)	73.2% (624)	68.9% (528)	69.7% (595)
Attendance	84.5	94.3	94.3	93.5		Limited English Proficiency	9.1% (91)	10.1% (94)	8.5% (72)	9.8% (89)
						Students With Disabilities	14.1% (141)	14.3% (135)	13.8% (119)	12.6% (116)
Demographic Makeup % (#)	2015-2016	2016-2017	2017-2018	2018-2019		Academically Intellectually Gifted	24.7% (247)	20.1% (187)	17.9% (154)	14.2% (131)
American Indian	0.1% (1)	0.1% (1)	0.3% (3)	0.3% (3)						
Asian	2.7% (27)	2.5% (23)	2.1% (18)	2.0% (17)						
Black	49.8% (498)	48.1% (445)	47.0% (405)	45.6% (424)						
Hispanic	27.0% (270)	30.3% (281)	31.2% (268)	32.0% (299)						
Pacific Islander	0.1% (1)	0.1% (1)	0.2% (2)	0.1% (1)						
White	17.3% (173)	15.6% (144)	16.0% (137)	16.8% (157)						
Two or More Races	3.1% (31)	3.3% (31)	3.1% (27)	2.5% (23)						

Suspensions

Suspensions (Short-term)	2015-2016	2016-2017	2017-2018	2018-2019		Suspensions (Restorative Practices)	2015-2016	2016-2017	2017-2018	2018-2019
# of Students OSS	110	89	91	119		# of Students RP	211	159	179	180
% of Students OSS	11.0	8.6	10.6	12.9		% of Students RP	21.1	17.1	20.8	19.5
# of OSS	150	125	135	187		# of RP	878	255	311	318

School Climate

Teacher Working Conditions	2015-2016	2016-2017	2017-2018	2018-2019		Student Climate	2015-2016	2016-2017	2017-2018	2018-2019
Teacher Working Conditions (TWC)- Overall	81.9	N/A	87.1	76.0		Student Climate - Overall	86.0	71.0	84.0	85.0
Teacher Working Conditions Response Rate	100.0	N/A	100.0	98.0		Student Climate Response Rate	96.1	95.9	96.0	95.0
Teacher Turnover Rate	2015-2016	2016-2017	2017-2018	2018-2019						
	15.5	20.0	19.7	TBD						

Student Achievement

6th Grade: End-of-Grade (GLP/CCR)	2015-2016	2016-2017	2017-2018	2018-2019		Performance Composite Overall	2015-2016	2016-2017	2017-2018	2018-2019
Reading	37.3/28.6	38.6/29.1	43.6/34.9	47.3/33.0		GLP/CCR	44.5/32.1	44.3/29.6	49.7/35.1	43.2/29.6
Math	27.5/23.9	33.3/28.1	40.1/35.6	47.6/28.7						
7th Grade: End-of-Grade (GLP/CCR)	2015-2016	2016-2017	2017-2018	2018-2019		Growth Index	2015-2016	2016-2017	2017-2018	2018-2019
Reading	39.4/28.3	36.9/30.0	42.0/31.1	46.3/37.2			Met/+1.1	Not Met/-2.2	Exceeded/+3.6	Met/-0.2
Math	33.0/28.0	32.1/27.5	38.6/27.7	47.6/35.5						
8th Grade: End-of-Grade (GLP/CCR)	2015-2016	2016-2017	2017-2018	2018-2019		School Performance Grade	2015-2016	2016-2017	2017-2018	2018-2019
Reading	31.5/22.0	33.7/25.8	35.3/25.7	37.5/26.0			52/D	49/D	60/C	51/D
Math (*EOG & Math I)	29.5/25.1	35.7/31.4	33.0/27.3	33.2/25.7						
Science	51.0/42.0	58.1/49.0	59.2/46.6	64.2/53.9						
Math I: End-of-Course (GLP/CCR)	2015-2016	2016-2017	2017-2018	2018-2019		English Learner Progress (#/% Prof.)	2015-2016	2016-2017	2017-2018	2018-2019
Math I	98.0/96.0	100.0/92.9	*	*			N/A	N/A	34/47.9	14/16.1

Data Analysis:

In the case of a large school district, it is strongly recommended that collecting and organizing be the responsibility of select central office staff members. Anyway, it is the responsibility of school leaders to ensure his/her staff have reliable data to make good decisions to move their school forward. In most cases, I have used SWOT analysis to guide my staff to make good use of the data at our disposal. SWOT analysis is a quantitative data analysis method that assigns numerical values to indicate strengths, weaknesses, opportunities, and threats of an organization.

Leaders, I urge you to be intentional when you are setting your school goals or establishing your strategic plan for your school. The proceeding SWOT analysis reflects a school in North Carolina that I have had the privilege to support toward the development of their strategic plan.

Strengths:	Weaknesses:
• Positive student-teacher rapport/student/teacher relationships	• Collaborative lesson planning
• Student engagement	• Broad vision of classroom structure
• Strong, knowledge educators, it was more student-centered, and less teacher centered learning	• Data-drive instruction
• Clear objective is posted	• Male teachers
• Teacher circulating through classrooms and assessing students through observations	• LatinX teachers
• Supportive	• Teachers don't stay long
• Small, friendly, family environment	• More group collaboration for teachers
• Student teaching	
• Engaged Learning	• Teachers were seated and not circulating classroom
• Monitoring student learning and progress	
• Print rich learning environment	• More efficient plans
• Teachers assess students	• Timing of data collected
• Productive school environment for learning	
• Raw data	• Lack of parent involvement
• Expectations	
• Outside perception	• More student-centered learning
• Opportunity to grow professionally	
• Provide welcoming environment	
• Kids want to be at school	
• Families of students stay throughout elementary to high school	

Opportunities:	Threats:
<ul><li>Commonalities</li><li>Can use rapport to foster learning</li><li>Cross-curriculum training, planning & instruction</li><li>Workshops, methods of teaching, more consistent</li><li>More PLC's for content level</li><li>PD training</li><li>Coding/Computer Science</li><li>Continuing education for teachers</li><li>Utilize culturally relevant lessons</li><li>Incorporate movement into lessons</li><li>Professional development</li><li>More collaboration between teachers</li><li>Use data to grow</li><li>Growth in all grade levels</li><li>Kinesthetic learning</li><li>PTA</li><li>Technology</li><li>Spanish learning for non-Hispanic teachers, staff, and students</li></ul>	<ul><li>Not being multi-dimensional in teaching strategies</li><li>Lack of diversity in student assessment practices</li><li>Standardized testing</li><li>Other schools offer electives and college ready classes</li><li>Limited planning time for teachers</li><li>Close-minded students & lack of participation</li><li>Children not reading/writing effectively</li><li>Teaching from the test</li><li>Low test scores</li></ul>

	<ul><li>Not retaining students</li><li>Outside forces</li><li>Lack of transitional skills/transfe rable skills</li><li>Mental issues-undetected</li><li>Economic threats</li><li>Racism and standardized testing</li></ul>

Goal Setting:

Goal setting should be a methodical process that goes from student data and teacher data to school data. A school should not set its yearly goal without properly counting every student in a unit that will be compounded to a school goal. Here's the process I have used in the past to establish a school goal:

Principal Mubenga is leading a high school with 1000 students, 9th-12th grades with 250 students per grade. In this school, only 9th graders and 10th graders will be taking the state assessments at the end of the school year. Principal Mubenga would like to set up the school goal for his incoming 9th graders and rising 10th graders. Principal Mubenga will have access to incoming 9th graders' last year's state assessment results and rising 10th graders' last year's results to establish realistic goals. The following graphs contain available data and the process of goal setting:

8th Grade Achievement Level Breakdown

Level	# of Students	% of Students
Extremely Below Grade Level	40	16%
Below Grade Level	60	24%
At Grade Level	125	50%
Above Grade Level	25	10%
Total	250	100%

60% of incoming 9th graders came to high school proficient. It is the responsibility of the school principal and teachers to maintain these students at or above proficiency levels and even help them exceed their proficiency levels. At no point should these proficient incoming 9th graders digress during the instructional year. Equally important, is the responsibility of the principal and staff to grow the 40% of students who entered 9th grade below grade level by establishing goals and creating a realistic way to aid these students to reach proficiency level. The administration should start by targeting the 60 students who are below grade level. In my common language, I call the 60 students *bubble students*. While setting goals for this school, the school administration should maintain the proficiency level of the 25 students +125 students + a percentage of the 60 *bubble students*. You can grow all bubble students to proficiency, or you can get most of them depending on the raw score and the plan of support to accelerate their learning. The extremely below-grade students can also gain proficiency with a plethora of supports. Beginning with 60% of these incoming 9th graders, the school can gain an additional 50 students which can easily derive from the 60 bubble students to grow the 9th-grade achievement levels to 80% proficiency.

Now, we are to view what happens at the individual classroom level by taking a look at the 80 students assigned to Mrs. Claire's 9th-grade class rosters. At the teacher level roster, the principal should have the list of students assigned to Mrs. Claire and use the same process of goal setting to arrive at a realistic goal for student proficiency levels. Each class's goal will be different depending on what the teacher will receive. However, the 80% goal should not change as the same tactics of setting goals will be consistent across the board.

Mrs. Claire's 9th grade classes

Level	# of Students	% of Students
Extremely Below Grade Level	0	0%
Below Grade Level	15	18.75%
At Grade Level	50	62.5%
Above Grade Level	15	18.75%
Total	80	100%

Principal Mubenga is expecting Mrs. Claire to maintain 62.5% + 18.75% proficiency and accelerate some *bubble students* to proficiency level while expecting all students to grow academically.

Mr. Smith's 9th grade classes

Level	# of Students	% of Students
Extremely Below Grade Level	22	25.88%

Below Grade Level	15	17.65%
At Grade Level	40	47.06%
Above Grade Level	8	9.41%
Total	85	100%

Principal Mubenga is expecting Mr. Smith to maintain 47.06% + 9.41% proficiency and accelerate some bubble students to become proficient while expecting all students to grow academically.

Ms. Johnson's classes

Level	# of Students	% of Students
Extremely Below Grade Level	18	21.18%
Below Grade Level	30	35.29%
At Grade Level	35	41.18%
Above Grade Level	2	2.35%
Total	85	100%

Principal Mubenga is expecting Ms. Johnson to maintain 41.18% + 2.35% proficiency and accelerate some bubble students to become proficient while expecting all students to grow academically.

Appendix I

Considerations for Building a Master Schedule Per Grade Span

Process of developing an elementary school master schedule

To build an effective master schedule for elementary schools, planning should start several months before the closing of the precedent school year. Planning early ensures that your team has analyzed all data sources from your school improvement goals and indicators. During the instructional planning process adjustments and alignments are implemented to ensure that the most effective, and experienced teachers are serving the students with the greatest academic needs. Planning provides teachers with more quality preparation and collaboration time during PLCs to make instructional shifts in instructional resources for students who are struggling. This time is valuable for principals to revisit instructional priorities, staffing assignments, student class placements, and subgroups' service delivery plans.

- Decide on goals for the next school year based on school data and School Improvement Goals

- Establish a Master Schedule Planning Team

- Define Roles and Responsibilities

- Review mid-year data (academic, MTSS tier 2 and tier 3 students, attendance, teacher, allotment, etc.)

- Prioritize the schedule for subgroups to determine the academic instructional need

- Ensure appropriate staffing and student placements based on student needs

The planning team should keep in mind that in the process of developing an effective master schedule, equitable student access to learning and resources should drive your master schedule. The first step to ensuring that all students have equitable access is knowing what students need. School demographic, academic/student learning, process, and perception data tell you what strengths and needs are in your school building in key areas.

Demographic data talks about who is in the school building. Are most or all of the students from low socioeconomic backgrounds? How many students are in the EC, ESL, or AIG subgroups? Academic/student learning data reflect what teachers are teaching and what students are learning. Which academic areas have the most need? What resources are needed to increase achievement in these areas? Process data reveals the processes and procedures in place at a school and how effectively they are running. Which processes need to be revised or implemented for the upcoming school year? Lastly, perception data conveys all stakeholders' observations about students' learning environment. It also reflects the attitudes and beliefs about the school. How do students feel about their teachers? Do parents believe they have a voice in the school?

After asking the questions about the key needs in the building, use the students' data and budget to determine which resources to purchase for those needs. Teachers group students in rosters according to common instructional goals and needs. Then, teachers choose the roster that works well with their teaching strengths. Rosters are balanced so that teachers can effectively manage students' needs and strengths. To ensure all students are treated with fairness, receive justice, and differentiated instruction, teachers provide at minimum an extra hour of small group time each week to students who have intensive and strategic needs.

- Determine student needs based on school data (benchmark, common assessments, pre-assessments, and post-assessments)

- Review sub-group school data (EC, ESL, and AIG)
- Create balanced rosters
- Match students' needs to teachers' strengths in all core areas
- Students' regrouping due to their needs
- Utilize the budget to purchase resources for students' needs

In conclusion, these six components are the vehicle to student success in building an effective master schedule. According to Thomas Armstrong (2012), "A strength-based classroom is a place where students with all sorts of labels come together as equals to form a new type of learning environment." Instructional leaders meet students' needs in master schedule planning when they prioritize setting high expectations for staff and students, strategically using appropriate support to target students' instructional needs, understanding the key instructional priorities, creating an instructional timeline, planning, ensuring equitable student access, implementing relevant, rigorous, and research-based instruction, implementing focused team data processes and procedures, and partnering with all stakeholders including parents/guardians.

Process of developing a middle school master schedule

Leaders:

To build an intentional master schedule for middle schools, you must consider several factors such as licensing and pairing teachers in teams based on strengths and chemistry. Here are the criteria to consider for an effective master schedule.

Use of Personnel

- The use of teams provides more support for middle school students
- Always consider the students' needs first when creating

their schedules.

- For example: a student who may need more behavioral support may need to be cross teamed to set the student up for success.

- The number of teams depends on the number of students per grade level.

- Teachers are placed according to their area of licensure and strengths.

- Strength example: your strongest science teachers should teach 8th-grade science.

- There are two types of teams

- Professional Learning Communities (PLCs)

- Proven strategy: pair a successful veteran teacher with a beginning teacher.

- Veteran will provide PLC, lesson planning, and classroom management support

- Beginning teacher will bring fresh ideas

- Grade Level

- Need a strong teacher as the grade-level chairperson

Constructing the Schedule

- Schedule should include common planning for PLCs and grade-level meetings

- PLCs 60 minutes 1/week

- Grade level 60 minutes 1/week

- Identify which teams and teachers will teach Academic Intellectually Gifted (AIG), Students with special needs (EC), and English Learners students (EL)

- The number of classes, depends on the number of students

- You must be strategic to ensure you maximize staff support

- EC schedules should be created first

- AIG students may need to take high school-level courses

- There may be some courses that your staff cannot teach

- Ex: Math 2

- If the class is online, when is it offered, and what is the length of the class

- This will dictate when each grade level has its core classes and lunch

- Identify when intervention will be held

- Whole school intervention vs staggered times throughout the day

- Core classes and planning periods

- Allow for 1 90-minute elective or 2 back-to-back 40–45-minute electives to allot teachers 80–90-minute planning periods

- Planning periods:

- When core classes are taught will depend on your student population. Here are some things to consider:

- 6th graders lose focus easily and may need to have electives mid-day to allow for a break: core-core-electives-core-core

- 7th and 8th graders are where most of your athletes are, so one of those grade levels will need electives at the end of the day so that when students are dismissed early for sports, they do not miss a core class. Most teachers like planning at the end of the day, so switching between 7th and 8th may be considered.

- Core classes should be at least 60 minutes

Process of developing a high school master schedule

Master scheduling is a sacred task that the principal should not delegate completely to other members. A good example of master scheduling is the school creates a scheduling team with specific responsibilities. The purpose of the master scheduling team is to prioritize students' needs, not the adult's self-interest. It takes a collaborative team effort to develop a good master schedule.

Principal's responsibilities:

Will assign members to the team; cast vision for the master schedule; review reports; make data-driven, final decisions; approve specific requests from faculty regarding planning, preferred courses, etc.

Assistant Principal's responsibilities:

Will collaborate with the team to create a Registration and Scheduling Master Plan; manage the scheduling process; ensure team members meet deadlines and execute tasks with fidelity; make reports and recommendations to the principal; provide support to team members in accomplishing tasks through advocacy, professional development, direct assistance, etc.; recommend the removal of team members for inadequate performance; create a matrix in collaboration with Lead Counselor and Data Manager; approves or denies changes to matrix/schedule; ensures that all deadlines are met as established in the Registration and Scheduling Master Plan; and execute tasks as requested by the principal.

Lead Counselor's responsibilities:

Will collaborate with counseling staff to devise a registration plan that will enable counselors to meet with students to select courses

85

and update each student's 4-year plan; analyze course tally report and make recommendations to Assistant Principal; analyze course conflict report to ensure singletons and doubletons are filled and minimize potential course conflicts; create a matrix in conjunction with the Assistant Principal; make recommendations to the Assistant Principal regarding the schedule each time the classes are filled with students; create a schedule that ensures a minimum of 90% of students are scheduled without exceeding classroom capacity; ensures counselors collaborate with department leads to ensure their specialty classes are scheduled for proper courses; and execute tasks as requested by the principal or assistant principal.

Program Coordinators' responsibilities:

EC Inclusion Lead—will collaborate with the scheduling team; will work with Lead Counselor and Assistant Principal to ensure students receiving inclusion services are scheduled in advance of the entire school; work with lead counselor and assistant principal to ensure that inclusion sections are balanced; work with EC Resource teachers before the end of the school year to verify all inclusion students are properly scheduled; and execute tasks as requested by the principal and assistant principal;

ESL Coordinator—will collaborate with the scheduling team; will work with the counselors to make sure ESL students have selected the proper ESL courses; coordinate with the lead counselor and assistant principal to create sheltered ESL classes where needed; work with counselors to ensure all ESL students are fully scheduled; and execute tasks as requested by the principal and assistant principal; EC Self-Contained Lead—will collaborate with the scheduling team; will work with Lead Counselor and Assistant Principal to ensure self-contained students are scheduled in advance of the entire school; work with self-contained teachers before the end of the school year to verify all inclusion students are properly scheduled; and execute tasks as requested by the principal and assistant principal.

Data Manager's responsibilities:

Will collaborate with the Lead Counselor, Assistant Principal, and Principal to ensure all data agreed upon by the Leadership Team by way of the Scheduling Team is entered into PowerSchool; input data as requested by the Lead Counselor and Assistant Principal; ensure correct courses are in PowerSchool; generate reports for the Scheduling Team when requested; seek feedback from Central Office to ensure we are using PowerSchool at its maximum potential where registration and scheduling are concerned; advise the team of potential pitfalls, historical perspectives, and other considerations; works with Lead Counselor and assistant principal to create a schedule that ensures a minimum of 90% of students are scheduled without exceeding classroom capacity; ensure that all students are scheduled by the deadline; and execute tasks as requested by the principal, assistant principal, and lead counselor.

Appendix J

Structuring PLCs

Educating students in a complex world requires effective professional learning communities such as action research, lesson study, and protocols that help educators reach the next level of excellence in their collaboration and practice. When educators collaborate in groups, protocols can help educators change the culture of the school so that all adults and students improve their learning.

Leaders, in my days of leading schools and consulting, the Tuning Protocol was my favorite. I have preached and modeled it, and it has been a great framework that guided our professional discussions because of these professional conversations, I have seen a drastic improvement in teachers' growth and students' learning. Here are the Tuning Protocol Guidelines:

The Tuning Protocol was developed by David Allen and Joe McDonald at the Coalition of Essential Schools primarily for use in looking closely at student exhibitions. In the outline below, unless otherwise noted, the time allotments indicated are the suggested minimum for each task.

I. Introduction [10 minutes]. The Facilitator briefly introduces protocol goals, norms, and agenda. Participants briefly introduce themselves.

II. Teacher Presentation [20 minutes]. The Presenter describes the context for student work (its vision, coaching, scoring rubric, etc.) and presents samples of student work (such as photocopied pieces of written work or video clips of an exhibition).

III. Clarifying Questions [5 minutes maximum]. The Facilitator judges if questions more properly belong as warm or cool feedback than as clarifiers.

IV. Pause to reflect on warm and cool feedback [2 to 3 minutes maximum]. Participants make note of "warm," supportive feedback and "cool," more distanced comments (generally no more than one of each).

V. Warm and Cool Feedback [15 minutes]. Participants among themselves share responses to the work and its context; the teacher-presenter is silent. The Facilitator may lend focus by reminding participants of an area of emphasis supplied by the teacher-presenter.

VI. Reflection/Response [15 minutes]. Teacher-presenter reflects on and responds to those comments or questions he or she chooses to. Participants are silent. The Facilitator may clarify or lend focus.

VII. Debrief [10 minutes]. Beginning with the teacher-presenter ("How did the protocol experience compare with what you expected?"), the group discusses any frustrations, misunderstandings, or positive reactions participants have experienced. A more general discussion of the tuning protocol may develop.

Guidelines for Facilitators

1. Be assertive about keeping time. A protocol that doesn't allow for all the components will do a disservice to the presenter, the work presented, and the participants. understanding of the process. Don't let one participant monopolize.

2. Be protective of teacher-presenters. By making their work more public, teachers are exposing themselves to kinds of critiques they may not be used to. Inappropriate comments or questions should be recast or withdrawn. Try to determine just how "tough" your presenter wants the feedback to be.

3. Be provocative of substantive discourse. Many presenters may be used to blanket praise. Without thoughtful but probing "cool" questions and comments, they won't benefit from the tuning protocol experience. Presenters often say they'd have liked more cool feedback.

Norms for Participants

1. Be respectful of teacher-presenters. By making their work more public, teachers are exposing themselves to kinds of critiques they may not be used to. Inappropriate comments or questions should be recast or withdrawn.

2. Contribute to substantive discourse. Without thoughtful but probing "cool" questions and comments, presenters won't benefit from the tuning protocol experience.

3. Be appreciative of the facilitator's role, particularly regarding following the norms and keeping time. A tuning protocol that doesn't allow for all components (presentation, feedback, response, debrief) to be enacted properly will do a disservice both to the teacher-presenters and the participants.

Due to time constraints, some schools will not have enough time to appropriate more than 60 minutes for PLC; for that reason, it is important to introduce the Modified Tuning Protocol which is more realistic to conduct during school hours.

Topic	Desired Outcome	Person Responsible	Time
Welcome	Introductions	Facilitator	6
Teacher Presentation	The Teacher Presenter describes the context for student work.	Teacher-Presenter	7
Clarifying Questions	Participants ask clarifying questions.	Team	6
Examination of Student Work	Share and review samples of student work	Team	10

Samples			
Warm and Cool Feedback	Remind participants of the focusing questions. Participants provide warm and cool feedback.	Facilitator, Team	8
Plan of Action	Determine action plan for Teacher Presenter.	Team	5
Debrief, Wrap up, Next Steps	Debrief and summarize outcomes.	Facilitator	3
		Total	**45**

What does PLC look like at the elementary school level?

The key for a group of teachers to work collaboratively is the need to have a common planning time. While their students are in elective classes or encore, that is the time for the professional learning community to take place. Some school leaders will ask their teachers to plan independently for two or three days and devote two days weekly to a PLC. Some school leaders would prefer a devoted day and time after school for all grade levels to concentrate on PLC work. PLC during school hours or after school depends on the maturity of your staff. If the school has protocols in place and each grade level has good facilitators, I always suggest this latest timing for PLC. With a clear protocol, you should expect teachers to discuss their lesson plans, student learning, assessments, students' data, and ways to improve student outcomes.

What does PLC look like at the middle school level?

At the middle school level, PLC can take place during planning periods or after school. I would suggest that you organize PLC groups in job-alike groups and mixed-job groups. In job-alike groups, teachers need to discuss students' learning and students' data and how to help them improve. In mixed-job groups, school leaders should organize PLC groups in subject areas for teachers to collaborate for content and vertical alignment. These mixed PLC groups can meet once a month to discuss pedagogical best practices. With clear protocols, the team should be able to have a productive PLC that would impact student learning.

What does PLC look like at the high school level?

At the high school level, PLC can take place after school. I would suggest that you organize PLC groups in mixed-job groups. In mixed-job groups, teachers need to discuss students' learning and students' data and how to help them improve. In mixed-job groups, teachers should discuss some pedagogical practices and different school initiatives that the school has for this academic year. With clear protocols, the team should be able to have a productive PLC that would impact student learning.

Appendix K

Benchmark Resources

<u>Bloom's Taxonomy Cognitive Domain for Teaching</u>

Your teachers must address all cognitive levels of the students through their instruction, challenging themselves to challenge students in their thinking and their production. A way to see whether teachers instruct students in addressing all the cognitive domains in their lessons. Listed below are the six levels of Bloom domains:

1. **KNOWLEDGE** represents the lowest level of objectives. The definition of knowledge for this level is remembering previously learned material. The requirement is simple recall. The range of information may vary from simple facts to complex theories, but regardless of the complexity, knowledge is the cognitive level being utilized by the brain. Examples of verbs or phrases to use to direct the desired learning task include: define, fill in the blank, identify, label, list, locate, match, memorize, name, spell, state, tell, and underline.

2. **COMPREHENSION** is the first step beyond simple recall. It is the first level at which we see demonstration and understanding of information. It is the ability to grasp the meaning of material. Examples of verbs or phrases to use to direct the desired learning task include: convert, describe, explain, interpret, paraphrase, put in order, restate, retell in your own words, rewrite, and summarize.

3. **APPLICATION** is the ability to show the pertinence of principles to different situations. At this level, students may apply concepts or methods to actual concrete problems. This thinking skill tells you that a student can transfer selected information to a life problem or a new task with a minimum of direction. Examples of verbs or phrases to use to direct

the desired learning task include: compute, conclude, construct, demonstrate, determine, draw, give an example, illustrate, make, show, and solve.

4. **ANALYSIS** requires more than knowledge, comprehension, and application. It also requires an understanding of the underlying structure of the material. Analysis is the ability to break down material into its functional elements for a better understanding of the organization. Analysis may include identifying parts and clarifying relationships among parts. This thinking skill tells you that a student can examine, take apart, classify, predict, and draw conclusions. Examples of verbs or phrases to use to direct the desired learning task include: categorize, classify, compare, contrast, debate, deduct, determine the factors, diagnose, diagram, examine, and specify.

5. **SYNTHESIS** requires the formulation of new understandings. If analysis stresses the parts, synthesis stresses the whole. Components of concepts may be reorganized into new patterns. A student can originate, combine, and integrate parts of prior knowledge into a new product, plan, or proposal. Examples of verbs or phrases to use to direct the desired learning task include: change, combine, compose, construct, create, design, find an unusual way, formulate, generate, invent, predict, produce, pretend, rearrange, reorganize, suggest, and visualize.

6. **EVALUATION** is the highest level of learning results in the hierarchy. It includes all the other levels plus the ability to make judgments, assess, or criticize based on evidence and clearly defined criteria. Examples of verbs or phrases to use to direct the desired learning task include: appraise, choose, compare, conclude, decide, defend, evaluate, give your opinion, judge, justify, prioritize, rank, rate, select, support, and value.

Hopefully, within three days, you will analyze a benchmark that is available to your school and teachers. Here are the steps to take for benchmark exam data analysis:

Benchmark Analysis Protocol

Norms and Expectations

- Individually review benchmark results before course-alike meetings.

- Participate in analysis and discussion.

- Be open to discussion.

- Suspend judgment long enough to examine the results rather than what we hope to see.

- Focus discussion on factors the school has direct control over.

Setting Context

1. Determine which standards were explicitly taught and assessed.

2. Clarify the purpose and ask a data question.

3. Assemble appropriate curriculum, instructional planning materials, assessments, and data.

4. Understand the roles, responsibilities, and expectations of all stakeholders.

Data Examination

1. Determine which standards were students more successful in and state the rationale.

2. Determine on which standards were students less successful and state the rationale.

Data Interpretation

1. Identify trends and patterns in the more successful standards

- What was the content and level of cognition of the standard?

- What materials/curricula were used to teach the standard?

- What instructional strategies were used to teach the standard?

2. Identify trends and patterns in the less successful standards

- What was the content and level of cognition of the standard?

- What materials/curricula were used to teach the standard?

- What instructional strategies were used to teach the standard?

- What product/process was used to measure mastery of the standard?

3. Identify trends and patterns in less successful test items

- What was the content of the incorrect test items?

- What was the level of thinking or cognition of the items?

- Did the students struggle with the content, level of cognition, or context of the item?

- What was it about the item that made the distractors attractive?

4. Identify trends and patterns of successful and unsuccessful student groups

- Were there some groups that outperformed others? What

were some potential causes?

- Were there some groups that underperformed others? What were some potential causes?

5. Identify what standards students need support in mastering based on benchmark data analysis.

Creating Data-Driven Action Plans

1. Determine when these standards will be retaught. When is the appropriate time to reteach based on the instructional pacing guide? Usually, I would recommend that if more than 50% of the class did not master the content, the entire lesson needs to be retaught. If less than 50%, the teacher should address the students who did not grasp the content in a one-on-one setting or via remediation opportunities.

2. Align the content and cognition of these standards to the appropriate curriculum and strategies.

- How can the curriculum support this?

- What instructional strategies are appropriate?

- Can you apply what is successful in the classroom to what is not successful?

- How will the reteach be different from the initial instruction?

3. Determine appropriate context for students to demonstrate that the reteach was effective

- What will the students do?

- How will it be measured?

4. Produce a data-driven Action Plan

DISSEMINATE

Share Solutions with All Stakeholders

<u>1. Share Action Plans with all stakeholders</u>

- Administration
- Teachers
- Students
- Parents
- Others

2. Monitor Action Plans

3. Share and Publish results

Exemplar of benchmark results analysis

Dear Leaders,

After working so hard to establish your goals, you must have a laser focus on your practices to ensure that you meet your target at the end of the school year. One of your practices is to ensure benchmark results correlate with your anticipated end-of-year results. The following data tracker can assist you in presenting your goals and your actual benchmark results.

School Data Tracker after benchmark

Teachers	Enrollment	Goal/ Target	Benchmark Result	Difference
Teacher A	20 students	15/20 = 75%	16/20 = 80%	(+5%)
Teacher B	20 students	12/20 = 60%	6/20 = 30%	(-30%)
Teacher C	20 students	16/20 = 80%	10/20 = 50%	(-30%)
Teacher D	20 students	9/20 = 45%	7/20 = 35%	(-10%)
Teacher E	20 students	18/20 = 90%	18/20 = 90%	0%

Teacher F	20 students	6/20 = 30%	5/20 = 25%	(-5%)
Total	120 students	76/120 = 63.33%	62/120 = 51.67%	(-11.66)

Pertinent observations:

- If these benchmark results were your end-of-year results, you did not meet your school goal.

- Benchmarks are supposed to be given as formative assessments so you can make necessary adjustments.

- You only need fourteen students to meet your goal.

- Teacher B and Teacher C are way off their targets. Are these teachers the problems? What support do these teachers or students need so they can meet your target? Do you need to assign some students from Teachers B and C to Teachers A and E? Can Teachers A and E move more of their students?

- If all these questions are properly answered and addressed proactively, the school will meet its projected goal at the end of the academic year.

About the Author

Dr. Pascal Mubenga has enjoyed a successful career in public education spanning over 28 years in North Carolina. He served as Superintendent of Franklin County and Durham Public Schools. He also served as a District Transformation Coach, a School Transformation Team Lead, and a School Transformation Coach with the North Carolina Department of Public Instruction for four years. Immediately preceding his work with NCDPI, he was the principal at Jones Senior High School in Jones County, North Carolina, from 2007 through 2011. Dr. Mubenga has also previously served as an assistant principal in Franklin County and a math teacher in Johnston County. He was also a math teacher at Chewning Middle School in Durham for three years. He began his career in public education as a math teacher for the Nash-Rocky Mount Schools.

Dr. Mubenga was sworn in as superintendent of Durham Public Schools on November 27, 2017, student academic progress and school performance both increased while the district strengthened its commitment to equity, inclusion, and the socio-emotional health of the whole child. Before the COVID-19 pandemic, the Durham community took notice, with DPS's enrollment growth in the 2019-2020 school year—by more than 500 students—for the first time in four years. Dr. Mubenga was honored by his peers in North Carolina as the North Central Regional Superintendent of the Year for 2020.

The foundation for this work was laid with the establishment of a 2018-2023 Strategic Plan to transform DPS and "ignite the limitless potential" of its students. Dr. Mubenga worked with a large group of Durham educators, community stakeholders, students, and families to develop the plan based on a rigorous data review and an early listening and learning tour of Durham County. The plan was comprehensive with clear benchmarks, prioritizing academic achievement, attention to the needs of the whole child, teacher and employee recruitment and retention, community engagement, and fiscal and operational responsibility.

Printed in the USA
CPSIA information can be obtained
at www.ICGtesting.com
LVHW051934270824
789430LV00001B/2